Charlotte Matthews 944D

10-

TRINITY
COLLEGE LONDON PRESS

Flute
Scales, Arpeggios & Exercises

for Trinity College London Flute & Jazz Flute exams from 2015

Initial–Grade 8

Published by
Trinity College London Press Ltd
trinitycollege.com

Registered in England
Company no. 09726123

Copyright © 2014 Trinity College London
Fifth impression (revised), March 2020

Unauthorised photocopying is illegal
No part of this publication may be copied or reproduced in any form or by any means without the prior permission of the publisher.

Photo: Zute Lightfoot, flute courtesy of Yamaha Music London

Printed in England by Caligraving Ltd

Initial

All sections to be prepared				
Scales & triads (from memory) – the examiner will select from the following:				
Scales: F and G major (first five notes only)	ascending and descending	min. tempo ♩=60	tongued	*mf*
Triads: F and G major		min. tempo ♪=120		

Scales

F major scale (first five notes only)

G major scale (first five notes only)

Triads

F major triad

G major triad

Grade 1

Flute candidates to prepare *either* section i) *or* section ii) in full				
either i) **Scales & arpeggios** (from memory) – the examiner will select from the following:				
Scales: F and G major E minor (candidate's choice of *either* harmonic *or* melodic *or* natural minor) **Arpeggios:** F and G major E minor	one octave	min. tempi: scales: ♩=72 arpeggios: ♪=120	tongued *or* slurred	*mf*
or ii) **Exercises** (music may be used):				
Candidate to prepare 1a *or* 1b; 2a *or* 2b; and 3a *or* 3b (three exercises in total). The candidate will choose one exercise to play first; the examiner will then select one of the remaining two prepared exercises to be performed.				
1a. A Sad Story *or* 1b. Rising and Falling	for tone and phrasing			
2a. Spiky *or* 2b. Snowflakes	for articulation			
3a. Symmetry *or* 3b. Waltzing	for finger technique			

Jazz flute candidates to prepare *either* section i) *or* section ii) in full				
either i) **Scales & arpeggios** (from memory) – the examiner will select from the following:				
Using the tonal/modal centre G: Major scale followed by major 7th arpeggio Dorian scale followed by minor 7th arpeggio	one octave	min. tempi: scales: ♩=72 7ths: ♩=60	straight *or* swung (♫ = ♩♪)	tongued *or* slurred *mf*
or ii) **Exercises** (music may be used):				
Candidate to prepare 1a *or* 1b; 2a *or* 2b; and 3a *or* 3b (three exercises in total). The candidate will choose one exercise to play first; the examiner will then select one of the remaining two prepared exercises to be performed.				
1a. A Sad Story *or* 1b. Rising and Falling	for tone and phrasing			
2a. Spiky *or* 2b. Snowflakes	for articulation			
3a. Symmetry *or* 3b. Waltzing	for finger technique			

i) Scales & Arpeggios

E harmonic minor scale (one octave)

E melodic minor scale (one octave)

Grade 1 continued

E natural minor scale (one octave)

E minor arpeggio (one octave)

F major scale (one octave)

F major arpeggio (one octave)

G major scale (one octave)‡

G major arpeggio (one octave)

G major 7th arpeggio (one octave)*

Dorian scale on G (one octave)*

G minor 7th arpeggio (one octave)*

ii) Exercises

1a. A Sad Story – tone and phrasing

1b. Rising and Falling – tone and phrasing

2a. Spiky – articulation

2b. Snowflakes – articulation

3a. Symmetry – finger technique

3b. Waltzing – finger technique

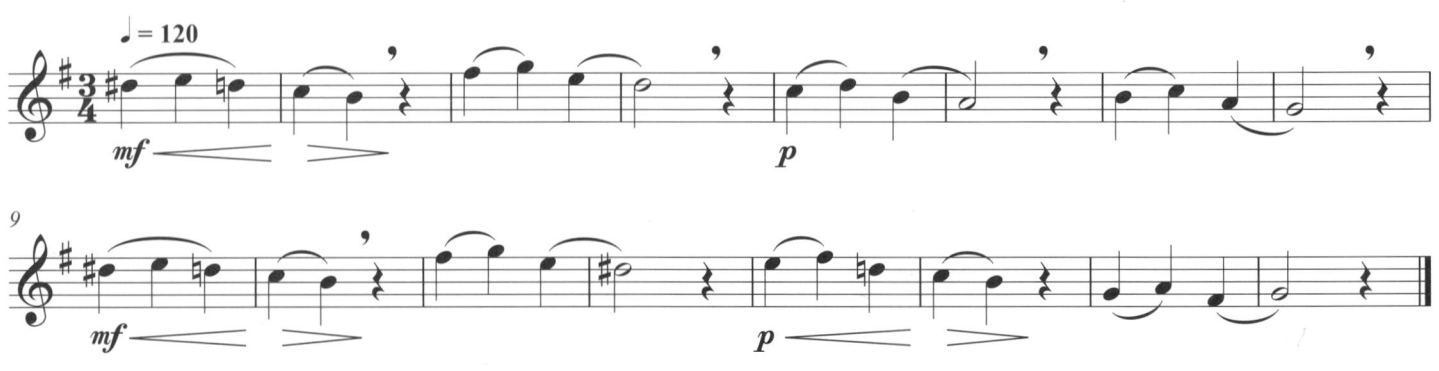

Grade 2

Flute candidates to prepare *either* section i) *or* section ii) in full

either i) Scales & arpeggios (from memory) – the examiner will select from the following:

Scales:			
D major	two octaves	min. tempi: scales: ♩=72 arpeggios: ♪=120	tongued *or* slurred *mf*
B♭ major A and G minor (candidate's choice of *either* harmonic *or* melodic *or* natural minor)	one octave		
Arpeggios: D major	two octaves		
B♭ major A and G minor	one octave		

or ii) Exercises (music may be used):

Candidate to prepare 1a *or* 1b; 2a *or* 2b; and 3a *or* 3b (three exercises in total).
The candidate will choose one exercise to play first; the examiner will then select one of the remaining two prepared exercises to be performed.

1a. Springtime	or	1b. Little Pinkie Waltz	for tone and phrasing
2a. A Conversation	or	2b. On Tiptoes	for articulation
3a. Swing Time	or	3b. A Minor Incident	for finger technique

Jazz flute candidates to prepare *either* section i) *or* section ii) in full

either i) Scales & arpeggios (from memory) – the examiner will select from the following:

Using the tonal/modal centre D: Major scale followed by major 7th arpeggio Dorian scale followed by minor 7th arpeggio Mixolydian scale followed by major arpeggio with a lowered 7th (D⁷)	two octaves	min. tempi: scales: ♩=72 arpeggios: ♪=120 7ths: ♩=60	straight *or* swung (♫ = ♩♪)	tongued *or* slurred *mf*

or ii) Exercises (music may be used):

Candidate to prepare 1a *or* 1b; 2a *or* 2b; and 3a *or* 3b (three exercises in total).
The candidate will choose one exercise to play first; the examiner will then select one of the remaining two prepared exercises to be performed.

1a. Springtime	or	1b. Little Pinkie Waltz	for tone and phrasing
2a. A Conversation	or	2b. On Tiptoes	for articulation
3a. Swing Time	or	3b. A Minor Incident	for finger technique

i) Scales & Arpeggios

D major scale (two octaves)‡

D major arpeggio (two octaves)

Grade 2 continued

D minor 7th arpeggio (two octaves)*

Mixolydian scale on D (two octaves)*

D major arpeggio with a lowered 7th (D⁷) (two octaves)*

G harmonic minor scale (one octave)

G melodic minor scale (one octave)

G natural minor scale (one octave)

G minor arpeggio (one octave)

D major 7th arpeggio (two octaves)*

Dorian scale on D (two octaves)*

A harmonic minor scale (one octave)

A melodic minor scale (one octave)

A natural minor scale (one octave)

A minor arpeggio (one octave)

B♭ major scale (one octave)

B♭ major arpeggio (one octave)

Grade 2 continued

ii) Exercises

1a. Springtime – tone and phrasing

1b. Little Pinkie Waltz – tone and phrasing

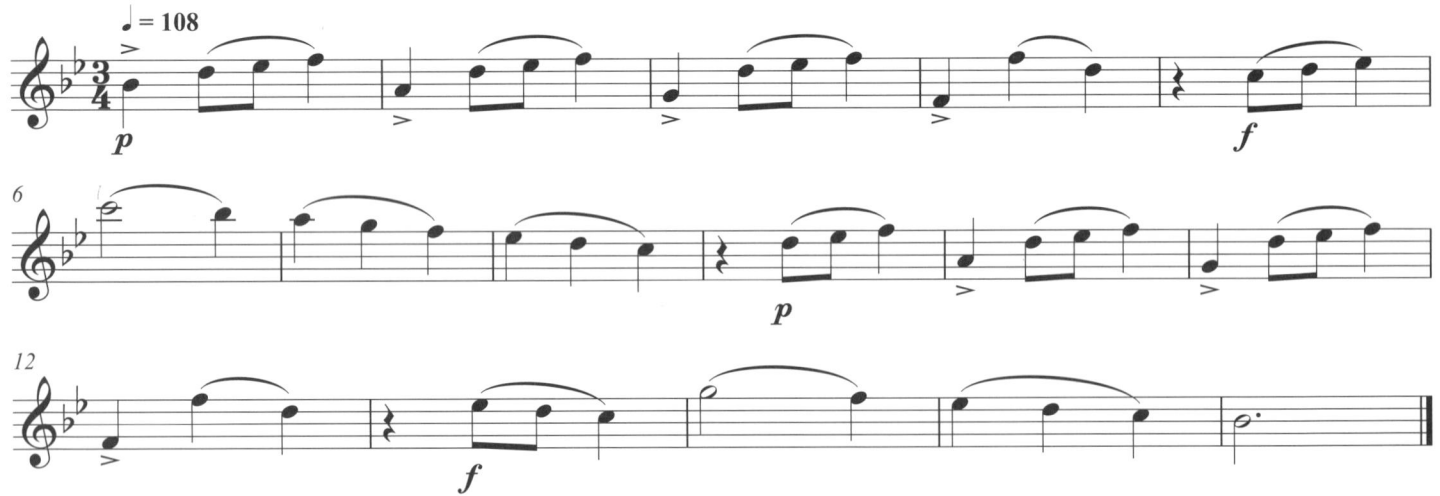

2a. A Conversation – articulation

2b. On Tiptoes – articulation

3a. Swing Time – finger technique

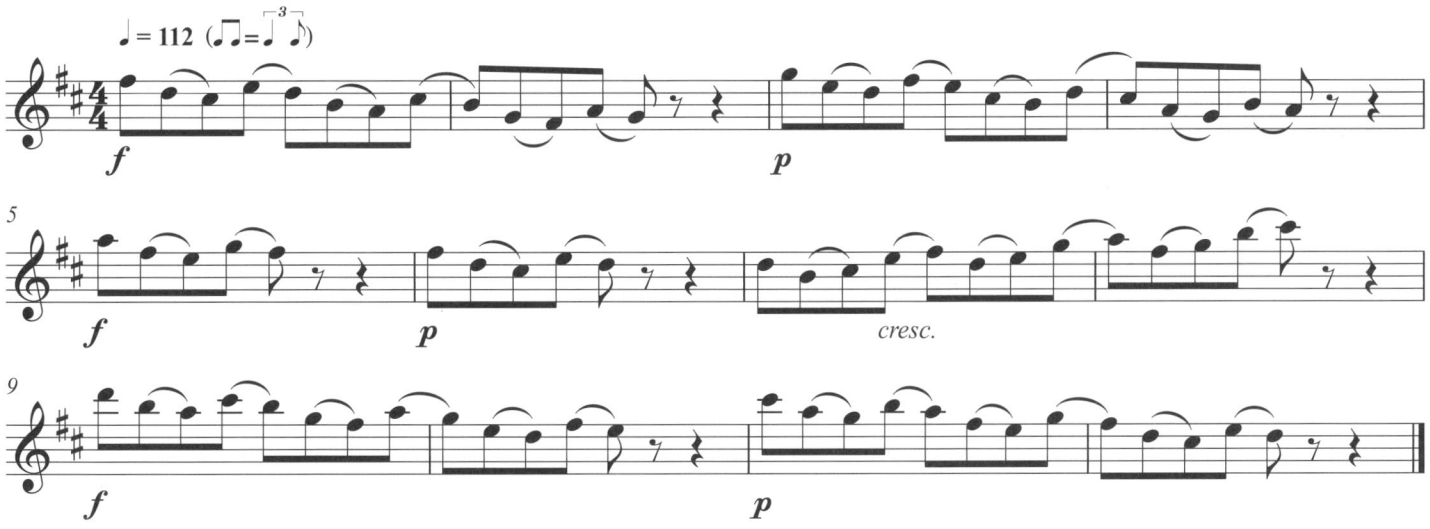

3b. A Minor Incident – finger technique

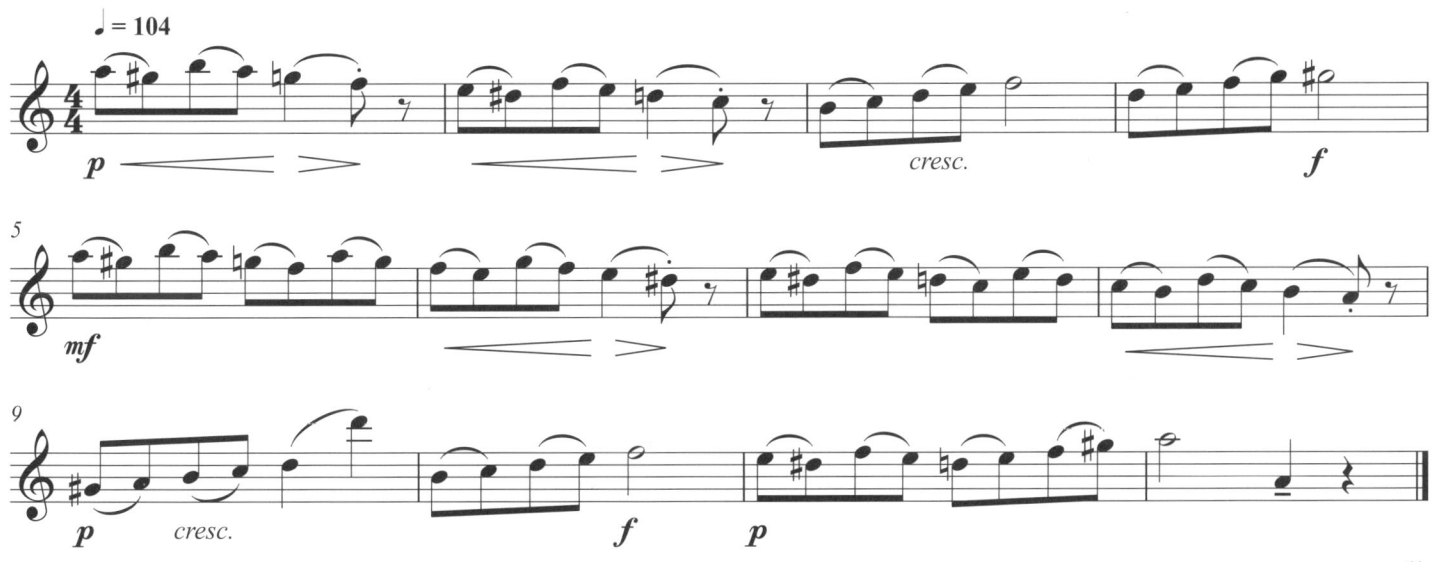

Grade 3

Flute candidates to prepare *either* section i) *or* section ii) in full

either **i) Scales & arpeggios** (from memory) – the examiner will select from the following:

Scales:			
F and G major G minor (candidate's choice of *either* harmonic *or* melodic *or* natural minor)	two octaves	min. tempi: scales: ♩=84 arpeggios: ♪=132	tongued *or* slurred	*mf*
A major A minor (candidate's choice of *either* harmonic *or* melodic *or* natural minor)	to 12th			
Chromatic scale starting on G	one octave			
Arpeggios: F and G major G minor	two octaves			
A major A minor	to 12th			

or **ii) Exercises** (music may be used):

Candidate to prepare 1a *or* 1b; 2a *or* 2b; and 3a *or* 3b (three exercises in total).
The candidate will choose one exercise to play first; the examiner will then select one of the remaining two prepared exercises to be performed.

1a. Persuasive	*or*	1b. Strolling	for tone and phrasing
2a. In the Groove	*or*	2b. Soaring	for articulation
3a. Sunshine	*or*	3b. Solitude	for finger technique

Jazz flute candidates to prepare *either* section i) *or* section ii) in full

either **i) Scales & arpeggios** (from memory) – the examiner will select from the following:

Using the tonal/modal centre A: Major scale followed by major 7th arpeggio Dorian scale followed by minor 7th arpeggio Mixolydian scale followed by major arpeggio with a lowered 7th (A⁷)	to 12th	min. tempi: scales: ♩=84 arpeggios: ♪=132 7ths: ♩=66	straight *or* swung (♫ = ♩³♪)	tongued *or* slurred	*mf*
Pentatonic minor scale	one octave				

or **ii) Exercises** (music may be used):

Candidate to prepare 1a *or* 1b; 2a *or* 2b; and 3a *or* 3b (three exercises in total).
The candidate will choose one exercise to play first; the examiner will then select one of the remaining two prepared exercises to be performed.

1a. Persuasive	*or*	1b. Strolling	for tone and phrasing
2a. In the Groove	*or*	2b. Soaring	for articulation
3a. Sunshine	*or*	3b. Solitude	for finger technique

i) Scales & Arpeggios

F major scale (two octaves)

F major arpeggio (two octaves)

Grade 3 continued

A major 7th arpeggio (to a 12th)*

Dorian scale on A (to a 12th)*

A minor 7th arpeggio (to a 12th)*

Mixolydian scale on A (to a 12th)*

A major arpeggio with a lowered 7th (A⁷) (to a 12th)*

A harmonic minor scale (to a 12th)

A melodic minor scale (to a 12th)

A natural minor scale (to a 12th)

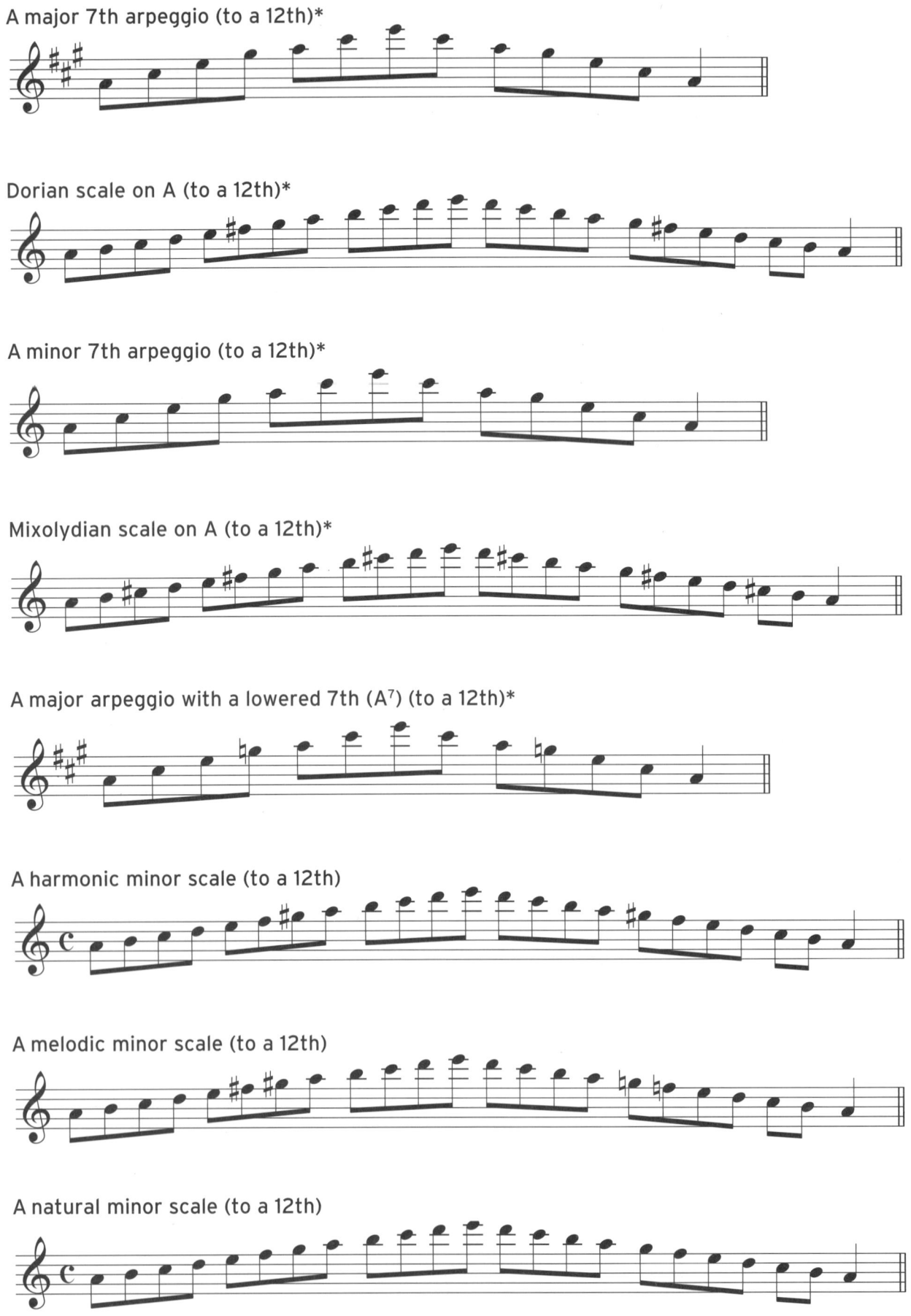

A minor arpeggio (to a 12th)

A pentatonic minor scale (one octave)*

ii) Exercises

1a. Persuasive – tone and phrasing

1b. Strolling – tone and phrasing

Grade 3 continued

2a. In the Groove – articulation

2b. Soaring – articulation

3a. Sunshine – finger technique

3b. Solitude – finger technique

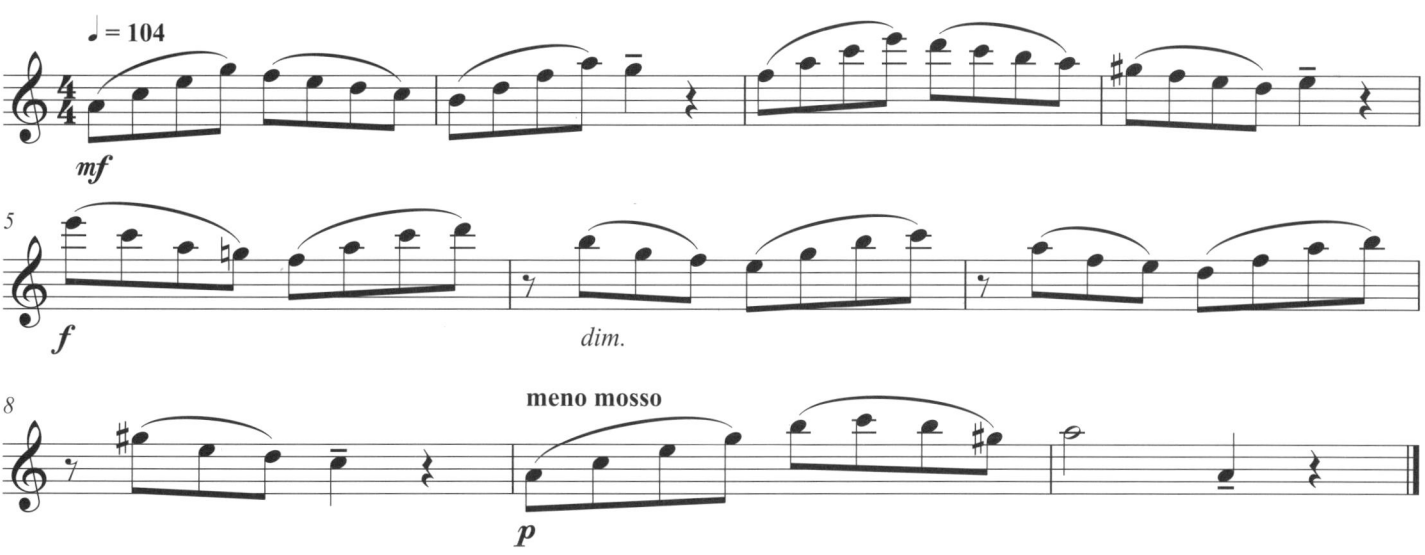

Grade 4

Flute candidates to prepare *either* section i) *or* section ii) in full

either i) Scales & arpeggios (from memory) – the examiner will select from the following:

Scales:				
C, G and E♭ major D and E minor (candidate's choice of *either* harmonic *or* melodic *or* natural minor)	two octaves	min. tempi: scales: ♩=96 arpeggios: ♪=138 7ths: ♩=69	tongued *or* slurred	*mf*
Chromatic scale starting on D				
Pentatonic (major) scale starting on D				
B minor (candidate's choice of *either* harmonic *or* melodic *or* natural minor)	to 12th			
Arpeggios: C, G and E♭ major D and E minor Dominant 7ths in the keys of C and G	two octaves			
B minor	to 12th			

or ii) Exercises (music may be used):

Candidate to prepare 1a *or* 1b; 2a *or* 2b; and 3a *or* 3b (three exercises in total).

The candidate will choose one exercise to play first; the examiner will then select one of the remaining two prepared exercises to be performed.

1a. Memories	or	1b. Sing It!	for tone and phrasing
2a. Groove in Blue	or	2b. Mechanical	for articulation
3a. Sighing	or	3b. The Machine	for finger technique

Jazz flute candidates to prepare *either* section i) *or* section ii) in full

either i) Scales & arpeggios (from memory) – the examiner will select from the following:

Using the tonal/modal centre C:				
Major scale	two and a half octaves	min. tempi: scales: ♩=96 arpeggios: ♪=138 7ths: ♩=69	straight *or* swung (♫ = ♩³♪)	tongued *or* slurred	*mf*
Major 7th arpeggio Dorian scale followed by minor 7th arpeggio Mixolydian scale followed by major arpeggio with a lowered 7th (C⁷) Pentatonic minor scale Melodic *or* jazz melodic minor scale followed by minor arpeggio with major 7th Chromatic scale	two octaves			

or ii) Exercises (music may be used):

Candidate to prepare 1a *or* 1b; 2a *or* 2b; and 3a *or* 3b (three exercises in total).

The candidate will choose one exercise to play first; the examiner will then select one of the remaining two prepared exercises to be performed.

1a. Memories	or	1b. Sing It!	for tone and phrasing
2a. Groove in Blue	or	2b. Mechanical	for articulation
3a. Sighing	or	3b. The Machine	for finger technique

i) Scales & Arpeggios

C major scale (two octaves)

C major scale (two and a half octaves)*

C major arpeggio (two octaves)

Dominant 7th arpeggio in the key of C (two octaves)*

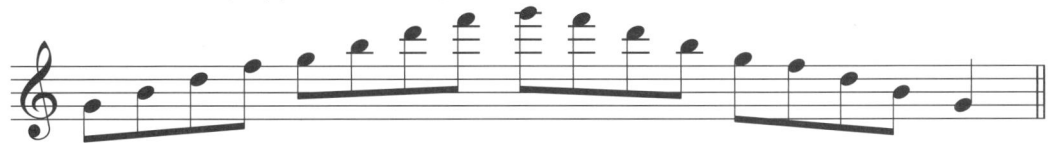

C major 7th arpeggio (two octaves)*

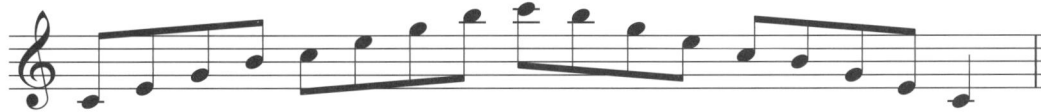

Dorian scale on C (two octaves)*

C minor 7th arpeggio (two octaves)*

Mixolydian scale on C (two octaves)*

Grade 4 continued

C major arpeggio with a lowered 7th (C⁷) (two octaves)*

C pentatonic minor scale (two octaves)*

C melodic minor scale (two octaves)*

C jazz melodic minor scale (two octaves)*

C minor arpeggio with a major 7th (two octaves)*

Chromatic scale starting on C (two octaves)*

D harmonic minor scale (two octaves)

D melodic minor scale (two octaves)

D natural minor scale (two octaves)

D minor arpeggio (two octaves)

D pentatonic major scale (two octaves)

Chromatic scale starting on D (two octaves)

Eb major scale (two octaves)

Eb major arpeggio (two octaves)

Grade 4 continued

B melodic minor scale (to a 12th)

B natural minor scale (to a 12th)

B minor arpeggio (to a 12th)

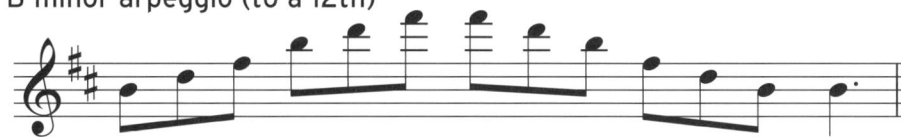

ii) Exercises

1a. Memories – tone and phrasing

Grade 4 continued

1b. Sing It! – tone and phrasing

2a. Groove in Blue – articulation

2b. Mechanical – articulation

3a. Sighing – finger technique

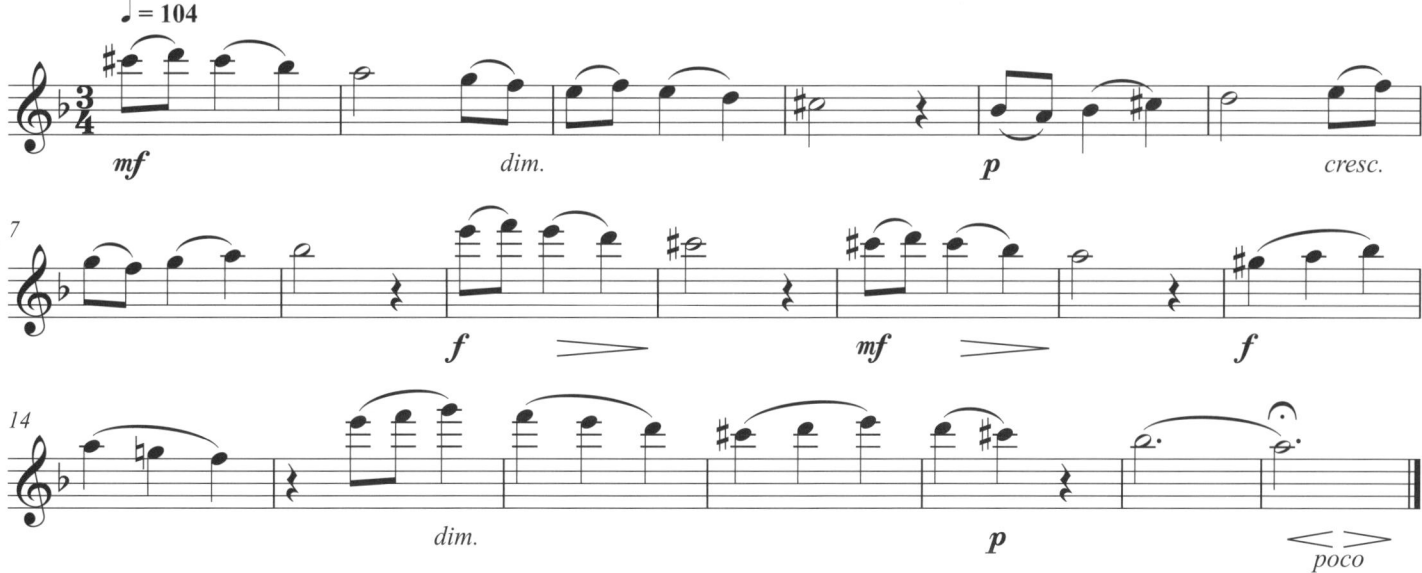

Grade 4 continued

3b. The Machine – finger technique

Grade 5

Flute candidates to prepare *either* section i) *or* section ii) in full

either i) Scales & arpeggios (from memory) – the examiner will select from the following:

	two octaves	min. tempi: scales: ♩=116 arpeggios: ♪=152 7ths: ♩=76	tongued *or* slurred	*mf*
Scales: A, E, A♭ and E♭ major C, F, C♯ and F♯ minor (candidate's choice of *either* harmonic *or* melodic *or* natural minor)				
Chromatic scale starting on E Pentatonic (major) scale starting on C (starting on lowest C)				
Arpeggios: A, E, A♭ and E♭ major C, F, C♯ and F♯ minor				
Dominant 7th arpeggio in the key of A♭ Diminished 7th arpeggio starting on F♯				

or ii) Exercises (music may be used):

Candidate to prepare 1a *or* 1b; 2a *or* 2b; and 3a *or* 3b (three exercises in total).
The candidate will choose one exercise to play first; the examiner will then select one of the remaining two prepared exercises to be performed.

1a. Shaping	*or*	1b. Reaching	for tone and phrasing
2a. Down Home	*or*	2b. Exploring	for articulation
3a. Crystal	*or*	3b. A Little Waltz	for finger technique

Jazz flute candidates to prepare *either* section i) *or* section ii) in full

either i) Scales & arpeggios (from memory) – the examiner will select from the following:

	two octaves	min. tempi: scales: ♩=116 arpeggios: ♪=152 7ths: ♩=76	straight *or* swung (♫ = ♩♪³)	tongued *or* slurred	*mf*
Using the tonal/modal centre of *either* E *or* F, at the candidate's choice: Major scale followed by major 7th arpeggio Dorian scale followed by minor 7th arpeggio Mixolydian scale followed by major arpeggio with a lowered 7th (E⁷ *or* F⁷) Pentatonic major *and* minor scale Chromatic scale Blues scale Diminished 7th arpeggio					

or ii) Exercises (music may be used):

Candidate to prepare 1a *or* 1b; 2a *or* 2b; and 3a *or* 3b (three exercises in total).
The candidate will choose one exercise to play first; the examiner will then select one of the remaining two prepared exercises to be performed.

1a. Shaping	*or*	1b. Reaching	for tone and phrasing
2a. Down Home	*or*	2b. Exploring	for articulation
3a. Crystal	*or*	3b. A Little Waltz	for finger technique

i) Scales & Arpeggios

C harmonic minor scale (two octaves)

Grade 5 continued

C melodic minor scale (two octaves)

C natural minor scale (two octaves)

C minor arpeggio (two octaves)

C pentatonic major scale (two octaves)

C# harmonic minor scale (two octaves)

C# melodic minor scale (two octaves)

C# natural minor scale (two octaves)

C# minor arpeggio (two octaves)

Eb major scale (two octaves)

Eb major arpeggio (two octaves)

E major scale (two octaves)‡

E major arpeggio (two octaves)

E major 7th arpeggio (two octaves)*

Dorian scale on E (two octaves)*

Grade 5 continued

E minor 7th arpeggio (two octaves)*

Mixolydian scale on E (two octaves)*

E major arpeggio with a lowered 7th (E[7]) (two octaves)*

E pentatonic major scale (two octaves)*

E pentatonic minor scale (two octaves)*

Chromatic scale starting on E (two octaves)‡

Blues scale on E (two octaves)*

Diminished 7th arpeggio on E (two octaves)‡

F major scale (two octaves)*

F major 7th arpeggio (two octaves)*

Dorian scale on F (two octaves)*

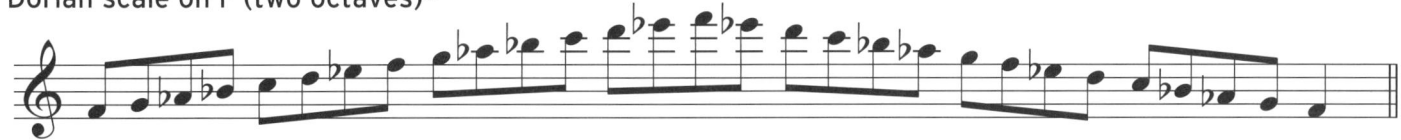

F minor 7th arpeggio (two octaves)*

Mixolydian scale on F (two octaves)*

F major arpeggio with a lowered 7th (F⁷) (two octaves)*

Grade 5 continued

F pentatonic major scale (two octaves)*

F pentatonic minor scale (two octaves)*

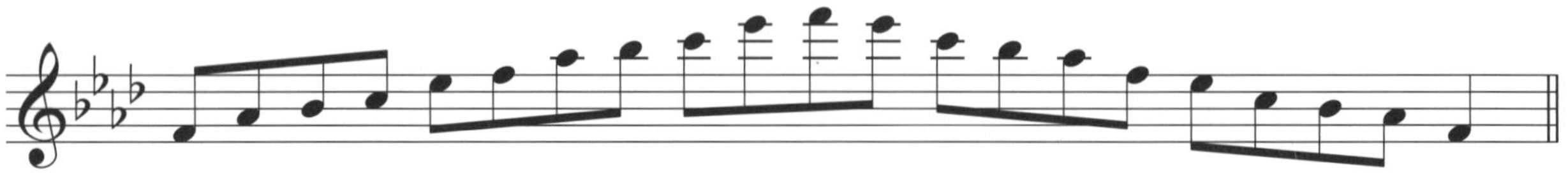

F harmonic minor scale (two octaves)

F melodic minor scale (two octaves)

F natural minor scale (two octaves)

F minor arpeggio (two octaves)

Chromatic on F (two octaves)*

32

Blues scale on F (two octaves)*

Diminished 7th arpeggio on F (two octaves)*

F# harmonic minor scale (two octaves)

F# melodic minor scale (two octaves)

F# natural minor scale (two octaves)

F# minor arpeggio (two octaves)

Diminished 7th arpeggio on F# (two octaves)

A♭ major scale (two octaves)

Grade 5 continued

Ab major arpeggio (two octaves)

Dominant 7th arpeggio in the key of Ab (two octaves)

A major scale (two octaves)

A major arpeggio (two octaves)

ii) Exercises

1a. Shaping – tone and phrasing

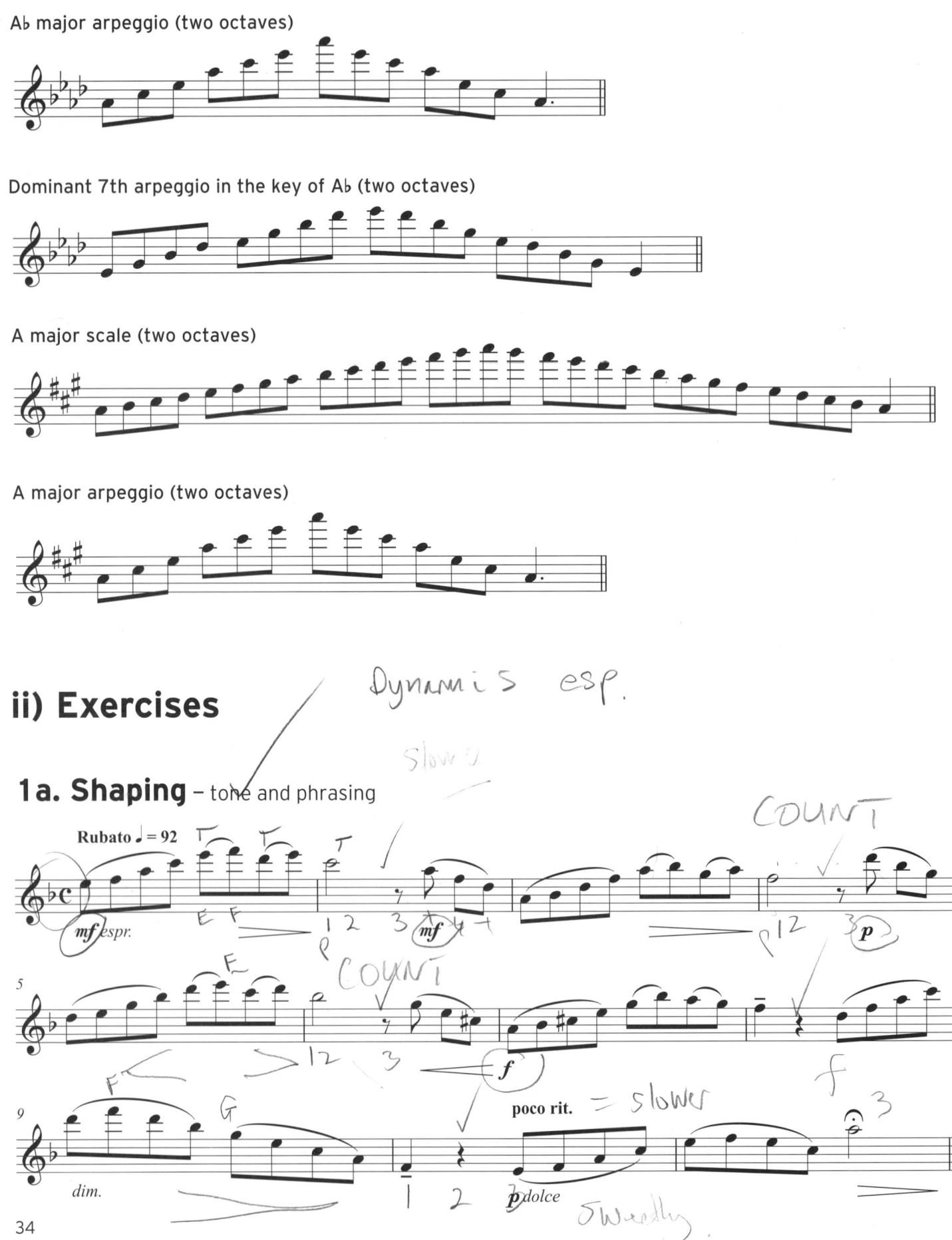

Grade 5 continued

2b. Exploring – articulation

3a. Crystal – finger technique

3b. A Little Waltz – finger technique

Grade 6

Flute candidates to prepare *either* section i) *or* section ii) in full				
either i) **Scales & arpeggios** (from memory) – the examiner will select from the following:					
Candidates should prepare scales and arpeggios from the following tonal centres: B♭ major, B♭ minor D major, D minor F♯ major, F♯ minor	two octaves	min. tempi: scales: ♩=120 arpeggios: ♩.=63 7ths: ♩=96	tongued, slurred or staccato-tongued	***f*** or ***p***
Plus: Pentatonic (major) scale starting on F♯ Chromatic scale starting on B♭ Whole-tone scale starting on D				
Dominant 7th arpeggio in the key of B Diminished 7th arpeggio starting on B♭				

When the examiner requests a major tonal centre, the candidate should play in succession:
   The major scale
   The major arpeggio					

When the examiner requests a minor tonal centre, the candidate should play in succession:
   The melodic minor scale
   The harmonic minor scale
   The minor arpeggio					

or ii) **Orchestral extracts**					
See current syllabus for details.					

Jazz flute candidates to prepare *either* section i) *or* section ii) in full				
either i) **Scales & arpeggios** (from memory) – the examiner will select from the following:					
Using the tonal/modal centres B♭, D and F♯: Major scale followed by major 7th arpeggio Dorian scale followed by minor 7th arpeggio Mixolydian scale followed by major arpeggio with a lowered 7th (B♭7, D7 and F♯7)	two octaves	min. tempi: scales: ♩=120 arpeggios: ♩.=63 7ths: ♩=96	straight *or* swung (♫ = ♩³♪)	tongued, slurred *or* staccato-tongued (straight scales only)	***f*** or ***p***
Pentatonic (major) scale starting on F♯ Chromatic scale starting on B♭ Blues scale starting on D Diminished 7th arpeggio starting on B♭					
or ii) **Study**					
See current syllabus for details.					

D major scale (two octaves)‡ – see Grade 2

D major arpeggio (two octaves) – see Grade 2

D major 7th arpeggio (two octaves)* – see Grade 2

D harmonic minor scale (two octaves) – see Grade 4

D melodic minor scale (two octaves) – see Grade 4

D minor arpeggio (two octaves) – see Grade 4

Dorian scale on D (two octaves)* – see Grade 2

D minor 7th arpeggio (two octaves)* – see Grade 2

Mixolydian scale on D (two octaves)* – see Grade 2

D major arpeggio with a lowered 7th (two octaves)* – see Grade 2

Whole-tone scale on D (two octaves)

Blues scale on D (two octaves)*

F# major scale (two octaves)‡

F# major arpeggio (two octaves)

F# pentatonic major scale (two octaves)‡

F# major 7th arpeggio (two octaves)*

Grade 6 continued

F# harmonic minor scale (two octaves) – see Grade 5

F# melodic minor scale (two octaves) – see Grade 5

F# minor arpeggio (two octaves) – see Grade 5

Dorian scale on F# (two octaves)*

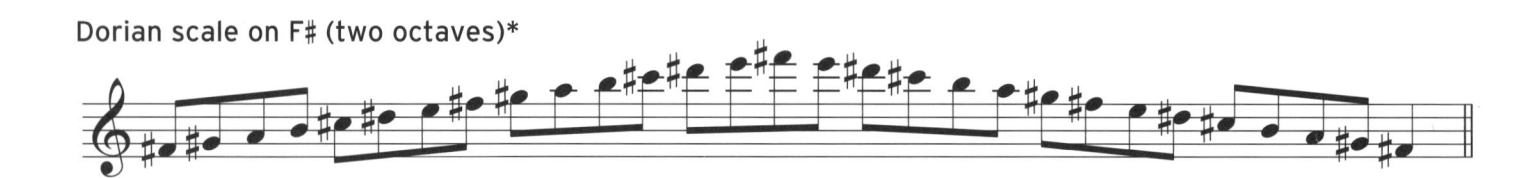

F# minor 7th arpeggio (two octaves)*

Mixolydian scale on F# (two octaves)*

F# major arpeggio with a lowered 7th (two octaves)*

B♭ major scale (two octaves)‡

B♭ major arpeggio (two octaves)

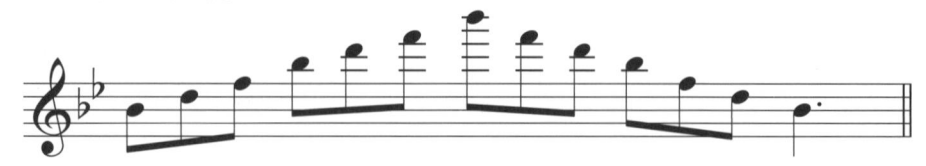

Bb harmonic minor scale (two octaves)

Bb melodic minor scale (two octaves)

Bb minor arpeggio (two octaves)

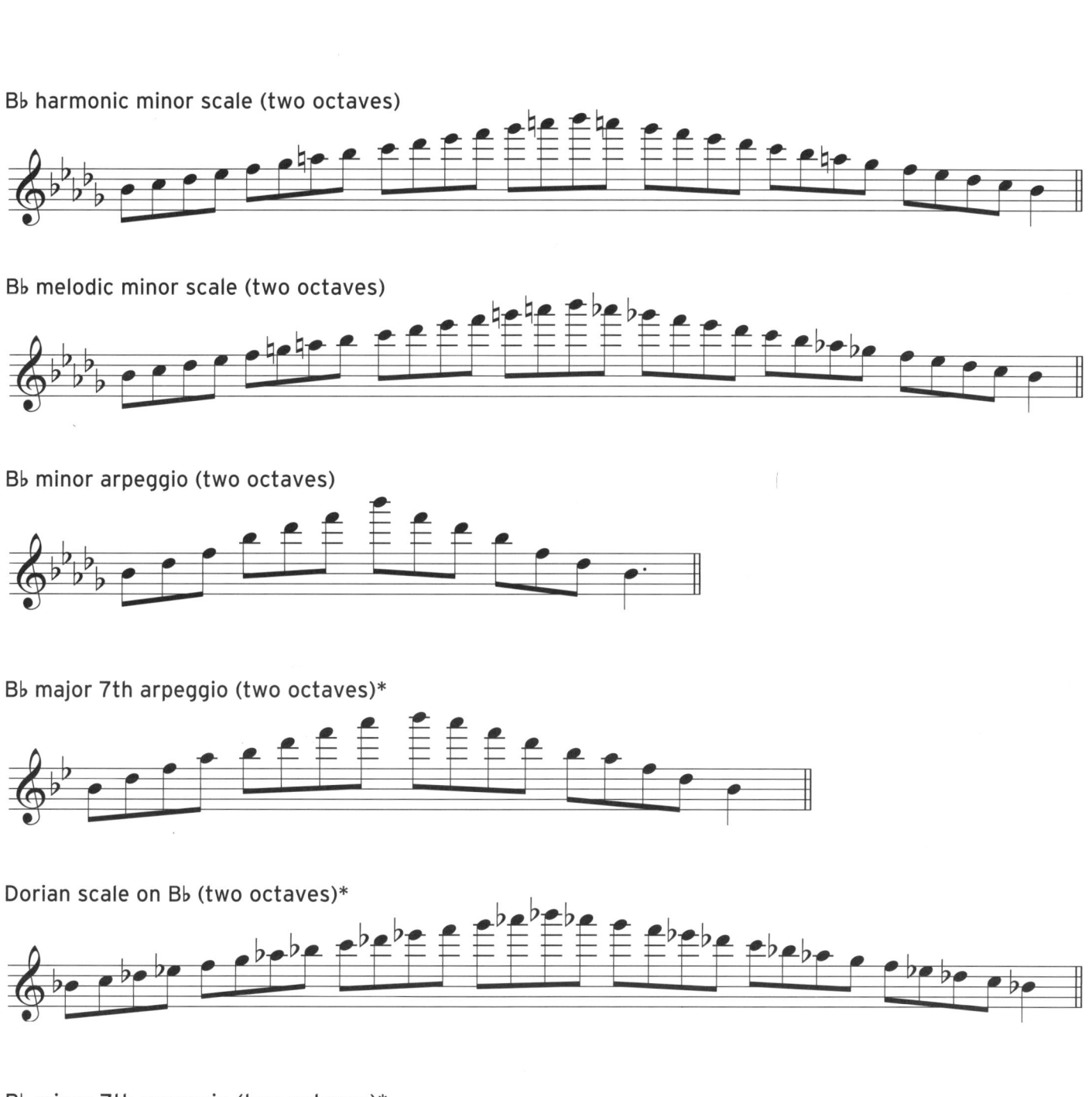

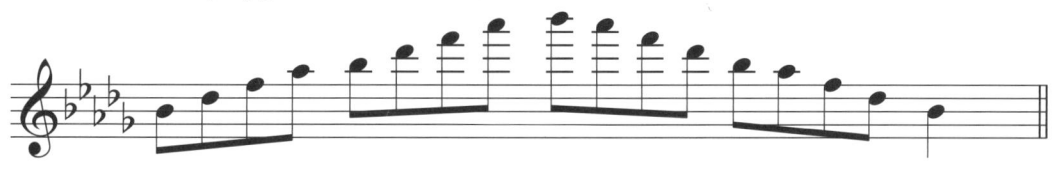

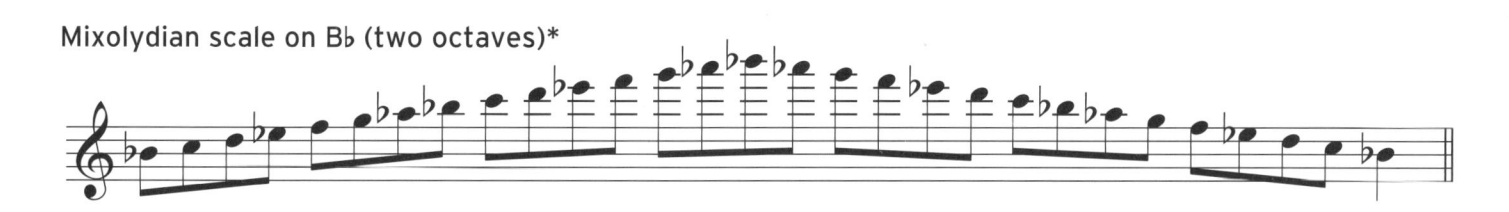

Bb major 7th arpeggio (two octaves)*

Dorian scale on Bb (two octaves)*

Bb minor 7th arpeggio (two octaves)*

Mixolydian scale on Bb (two octaves)*

Grade 6 continued

B♭ major arpeggio with a lowered 7th (two octaves)*

Chromatic scale starting on B♭ (two octaves)‡

Diminished 7th arpeggio on B♭ (two octaves)‡

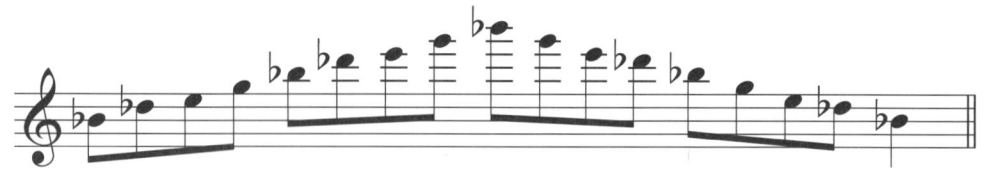

Dominant 7th arpeggio in the key of B (two octaves)

Grade 7

Flute candidates to prepare *either* section i) *or* section ii) in full

either i) Scales & arpeggios (from memory) – the examiner will select from the following:

Candidates should prepare scales and arpeggios from the following tonal centres: B major, B minor E♭ major, E♭ minor G major, G minor A major, A minor Plus: Chromatic scale starting on B Pentatonic (major) scale starting on E♭ and A Whole-tone scale starting on A Dominant 7th arpeggio in the keys of A♭ and D Diminished 7th arpeggio starting on B Augmented arpeggio starting on G	two octaves	min. tempi: scales: ♩=132 arpeggios: ♩.=69 7ths: ♩=104	tongued, slurred or staccato-tongued	*f* or *p*

When the examiner requests a major tonal centre, the candidate should play in succession:
- The major scale
- The major arpeggio

When the examiner requests a minor tonal centre, the candidate should play in succession:
- The melodic minor scale
- The harmonic minor scale
- The minor arpeggio

or ii) Orchestral extracts

See current syllabus for details.

Jazz flute candidates to prepare *either* section i) *or* section ii) in full

either i) Scales & arpeggios (from memory) – the examiner will select from the following:

Using the tonal/modal centres B, E♭ and G: Major scale followed by major 7th arpeggio Dorian scale followed by minor 7th arpeggio Mixolydian scale followed by major arpeggio with a lowered 7th (B⁷, E♭⁷ and G⁷)	two octaves	min. tempi: scales: ♩=132 arpeggios: ♩.=69 7ths: ♩=104	straight *or* swung (♫ = ♩♪)	tongued, slurred *or* staccato-tongued (straight scales only)	*f* or *p*
Using the tonal centre B: Jazz melodic minor scale followed by minor arpeggio with major 7th				
Using the tonal centre G: Whole tone scale followed by augmented arpeggio				
Pentatonic (major) scale starting on E♭ Pentatonic (minor) scale starting on G Chromatic scale starting on B Blues scale starting on E♭ Diminished 7th arpeggio starting on B				

or ii) Study

See current syllabus for details.

Dominant 7th arpeggio in the key of D (two octaves)

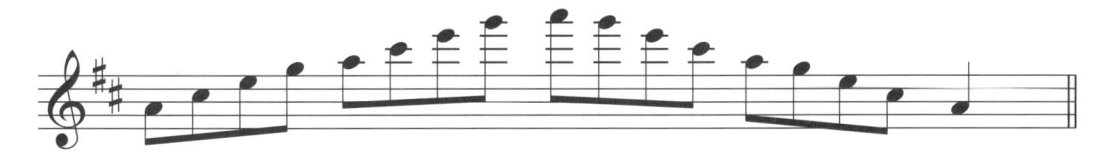

Grade 7 continued

Eb major scale (two octaves)‡ – see Grade 4

Eb major arpeggio (two octaves) – see Grade 4

Eb pentatonic major scale (two octaves)‡

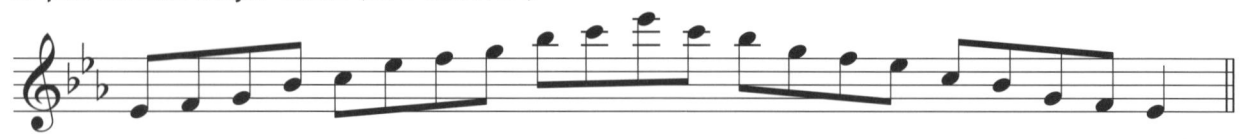

Eb major 7th arpeggio (two octaves)*

Eb harmonic minor scale (two octaves)

Eb melodic minor scale (two octaves)

Eb minor arpeggio (two octaves)

Dorian scale on Eb (two octaves)*

Eb minor 7th arpeggio (two octaves)*

Mixolydian scale on Eb (two octaves)*

Eb major arpeggio with a lowered 7th (two octaves)

Blues scale on Eb (two octaves)*

G major scale (two octaves)‡ – see Grade 3

G major arpeggio (two octaves) – see Grade 3

G major 7th arpeggio (two octaves)*

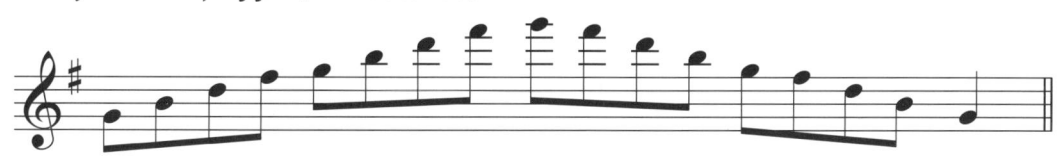

G harmonic minor scale (two octaves) – see Grade 3

G melodic minor scale (two octaves) – see Grade 3

G minor arpeggio (two octaves) – see Grade 3

Whole-tone scale on G (two octaves)

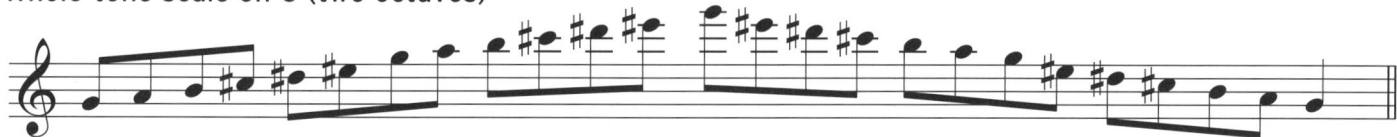

Augmented arpeggio on G (two octaves)*

G pentatonic minor scale (two octaves)*

Dorian scale on G (two octaves)*

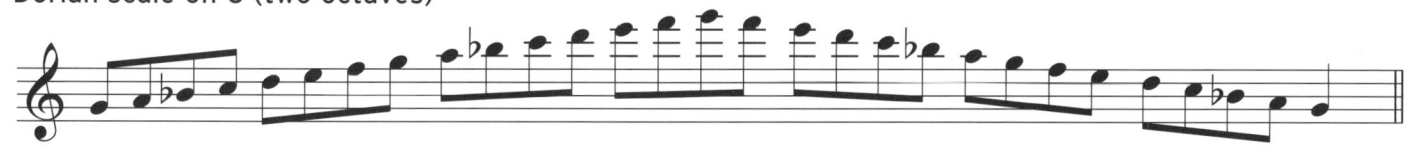

Grade 7 continued

G minor 7th arpeggio (two octaves)*

Mixolydian scale on G (two octaves)*

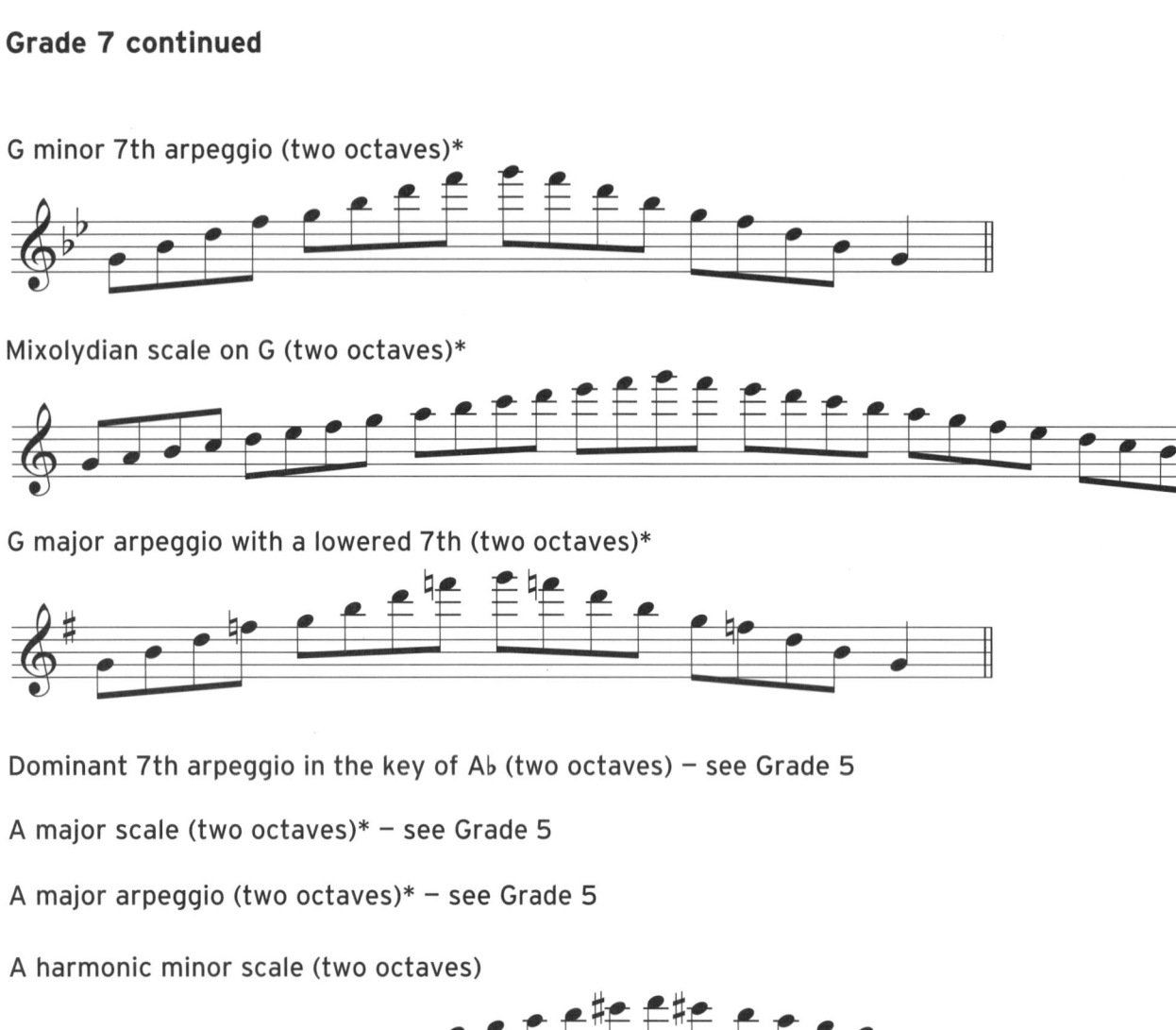

G major arpeggio with a lowered 7th (two octaves)*

Dominant 7th arpeggio in the key of A♭ (two octaves) – see Grade 5

A major scale (two octaves)* – see Grade 5

A major arpeggio (two octaves)* – see Grade 5

A harmonic minor scale (two octaves)

A melodic minor scale (two octaves)‡

A minor arpeggio (two octaves)

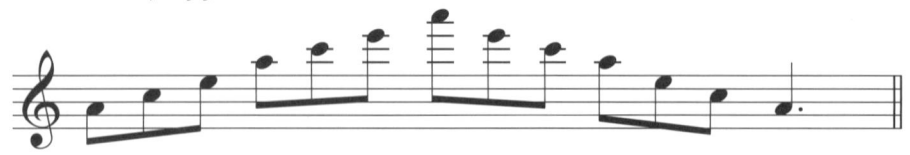

A pentatonic major scale (two octaves)*

Whole-tone scale on A (two octaves)

B major scale (two octaves)

B major arpeggio (two octaves)

B major 7th arpeggio (two octaves)*

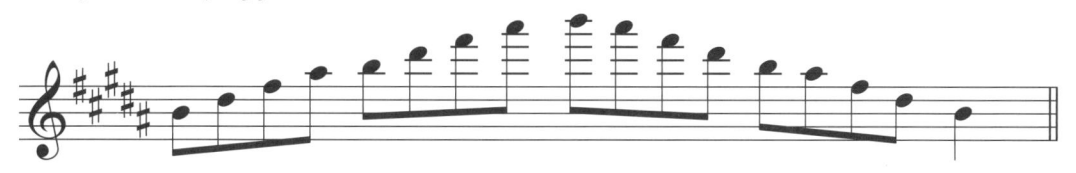

B harmonic minor scale (two octaves)

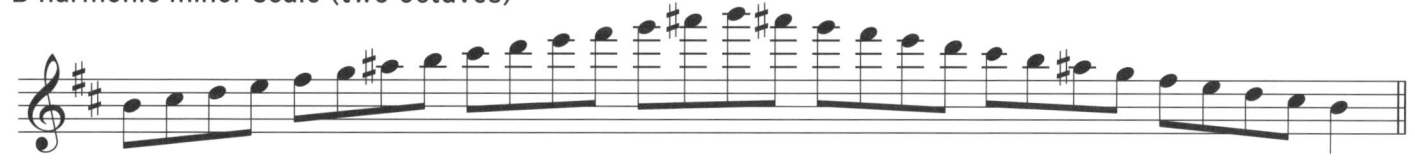

B melodic minor scale (two octaves)

B minor arpeggio (two octaves)

Dorian scale on B (two octaves)*

Grade 7 continued

B minor 7th arpeggio (two octaves)*

Mixolydian scale on B (two octaves)*

B major arpeggio with a lowered 7th (two octaves)*

B jazz melodic minor scale (two octaves)*

B minor arpeggio with a major 7th (two octaves)*

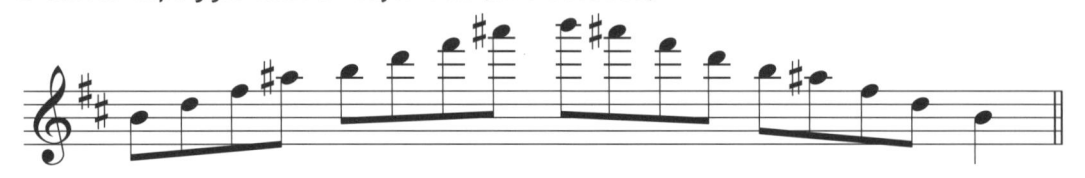

Diminished 7th arpeggio on B (two octaves)‡

Chromatic scale starting on B (two octaves)*

Grade 8

Flute candidates to prepare *either* section i) *or* section ii) in full

either i) Scales & arpeggios (from memory) – the examiner will select from the following:

Candidates should prepare scales and arpeggios from the following tonal centres: C major, C minor	three octaves	min. tempi: scales: ♩=132 arpeggios: ♩.=69 7ths: ♩=104	tongued, slurred, staccato-tongued *or* using mixed articulation*	*f* or *p*
E major, E minor A♭ major, G♯ minor F major, F minor D♭ major, C♯ minor	two octaves			
Plus: Chromatic scale starting on C Dominant 7th arpeggio in the key of F Diminished 7th arpeggio starting on C	three octaves			
Pentatonic (major) scale starting on A♭ Whole-tone scale starting on C♯ Dominant 7th arpeggio in the key of F♯ Diminished 7th arpeggio starting on A♭ Augmented arpeggio starting on E and F	two octaves			

When the examiner requests a major tonal centre, the candidate should play in succession:
  The major scale
  The major arpeggio

When the examiner requests a minor tonal centre, the candidate should play in succession:
  The melodic minor scale
  The harmonic minor scale
  The minor arpeggio

***or* ii) Orchestral extracts**
See current syllabus for details.

Jazz flute candidates to prepare *either* section i) *or* section ii) in full

either i) Scales & arpeggios (from memory) – the examiner will select from the following:

Using the tonal/modal centres C, E, A♭/G♯ and C♯/D♭: Major scale followed by major 7th arpeggio Dorian scale followed by minor 7th arpeggio Mixolydian scale followed by major arpeggio with a lowered 7th (C^7, E^7, A♭^{7} and D♭^{7})	C: three octaves E, A♭/G♯ and C♯/D♭: two octaves	min. tempi: scales: ♩=132 arpeggios: ♩.=69 7ths: ♩=104	straight *or* swung (♫ = ♩♪)	tongued, slurred *or* staccato-tongued (straight scales only)	*f* or *p*
Using the tonal centre C: Jazz melodic minor scale followed by minor arpeggio with major 7th	three octaves			
Using the tonal centre E: Whole tone scale followed by augmented arpeggio	two octaves			
Chromatic scale starting on C Diminished 7th arpeggio starting on C	three octaves			
Pentatonic (major) scale starting on A♭ Pentatonic (minor) scale starting on E Blues scale starting on C♯	two octaves			

***or* ii) Study**
See current syllabus for details.

*Mixed articulation scales and arpeggios to be prepared with the following articulation:

Grade 8 continued

C major scale (three octaves)

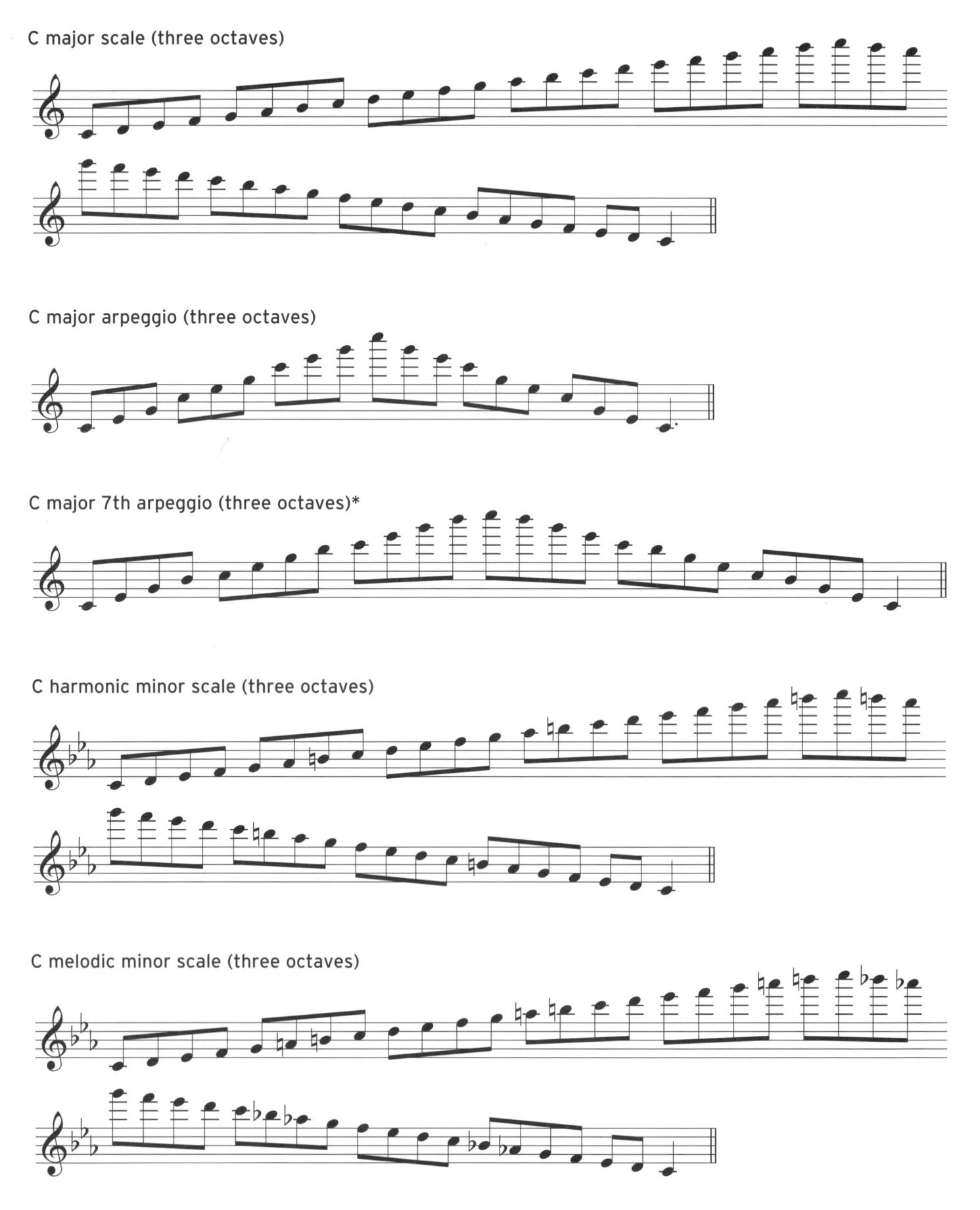

C major arpeggio (three octaves)

C major 7th arpeggio (three octaves)*

C harmonic minor scale (three octaves)

C melodic minor scale (three octaves)

C minor arpeggio (three octaves)

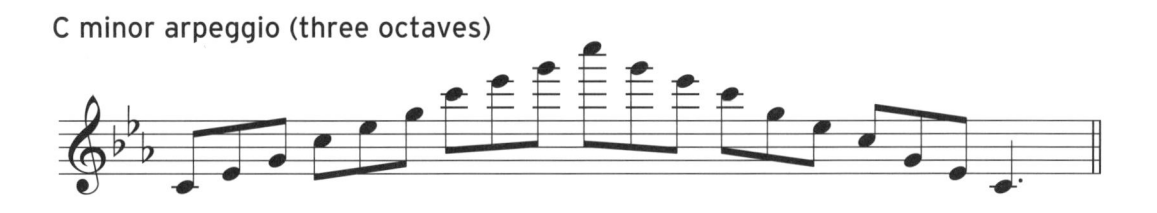

Dorian scale on C (three octaves)*

C minor 7th arpeggio (three octaves)*

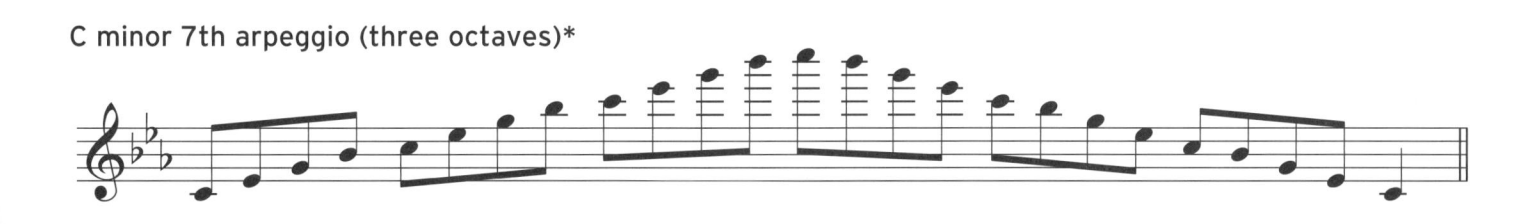

Mixolydian scale on C (three octaves)*

C major arpeggio with a lowered 7th (three octaves)*

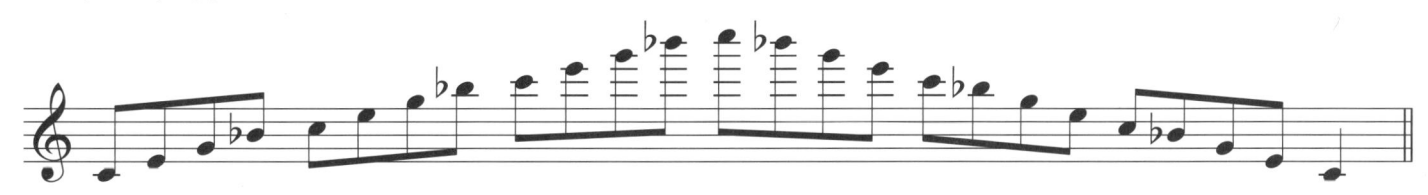

Grade 8 continued

C jazz melodic minor scale (three octaves)*

C minor arpeggio with a major 7th (three octaves)*

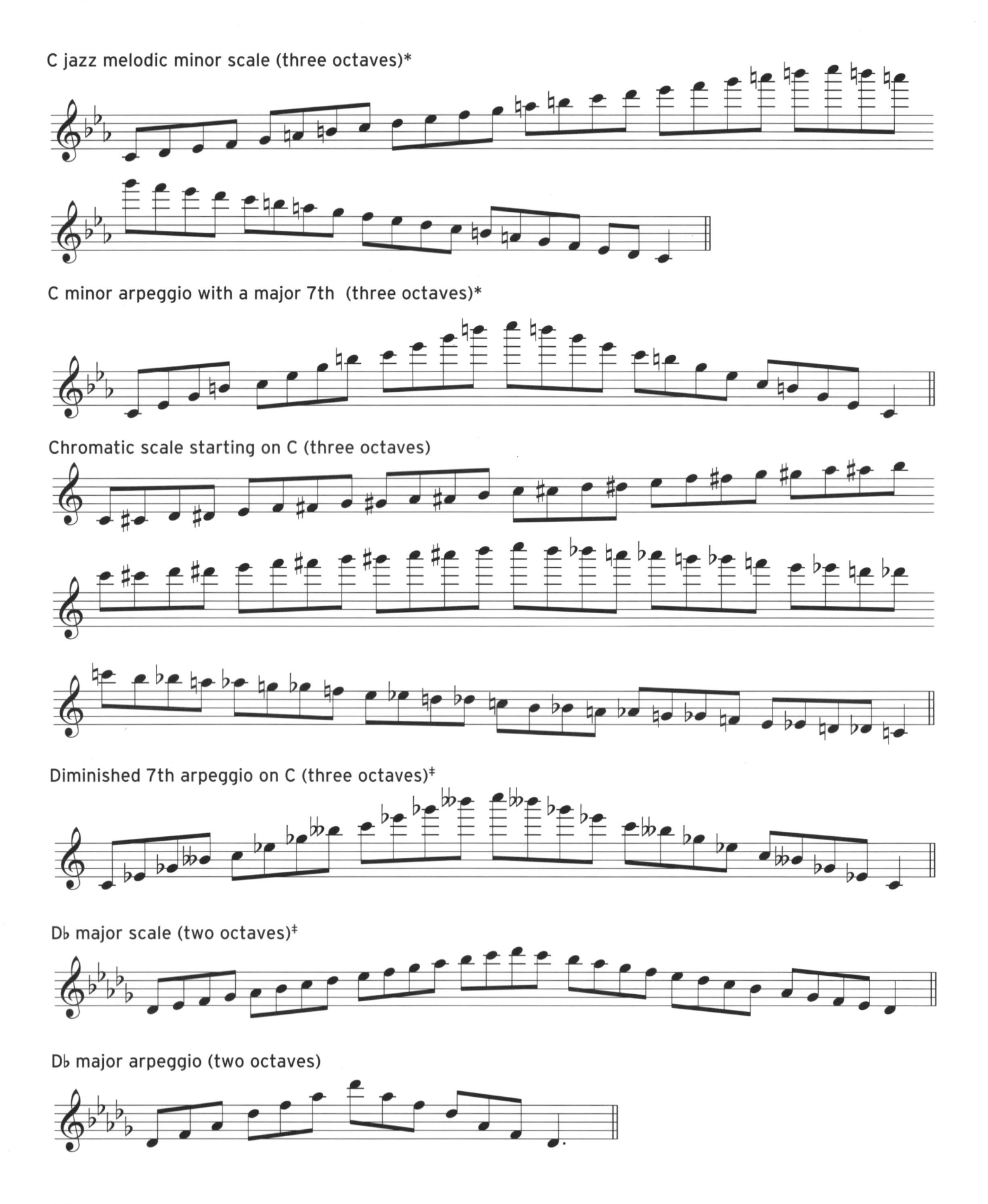

Chromatic scale starting on C (three octaves)

Diminished 7th arpeggio on C (three octaves)‡

D♭ major scale (two octaves)‡

D♭ major arpeggio (two octaves)

D♭/C♯ major 7th arpeggio (two octaves)*

C♯ harmonic minor scale (two octaves) – see Grade 5

C♯ melodic minor scale (two octaves) – see Grade 5

C♯ minor arpeggio (two octaves) – see Grade 5

Dorian scale on C♯/D♭ (two octaves)*

C♯ minor 7th arpeggio (two octaves)*

Mixolydian scale on C♯/D♭ (two octaves)*

D♭ major arpeggio with a lowered 7th (two octaves)*

Blues scale on C♯ (two octaves)*

Whole-tone scale on C♯ (two octaves)

Grade 8 continued

E major scale (two octaves)‡ – see Grade 5

E major arpeggio (two octaves) – see Grade 5

E major 7th arpeggio (two octaves)* – see Grade 5

Augmented arpeggio on E (two octaves)*

Whole-tone scale on E (two octaves)

E harmonic minor scale (two octaves) – see Grade 4

E melodic minor scale (two octaves) – see Grade 4

E minor arpeggio (two octaves) – see Grade 4

Dorian scale on E (two octaves)* – see Grade 5

E minor 7th arpeggio (two octaves)* – see Grade 5

Mixolydian scale on E (two octaves)* – see Grade 5

E major arpeggio with a lowered 7th (two octaves)* – see Grade 5

E pentatonic minor (two octaves)* – see Grade 5

F major scale (two octaves) – see Grade 5

F major arpeggio (two octaves) – see Grade 5

F harmonic minor (two octaves) – see Grade 5

F melodic minor (two octaves) – see Grade 5

F minor arpeggio (two octaves) – see Grade 5

Augmented arpeggio on F (two octaves)

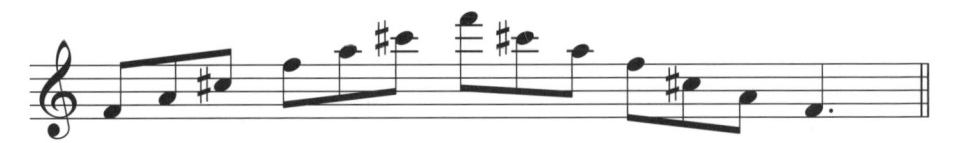

Dominant 7th arpeggio in the key of F (three octaves)

Dominant 7th arpeggio in the key of F# (two octaves)

A♭ major scale (two octaves)‡ – see Grade 5

A♭ major arpeggio (two octaves) – see Grade 5

A♭ major 7th arpeggio (two octaves)*

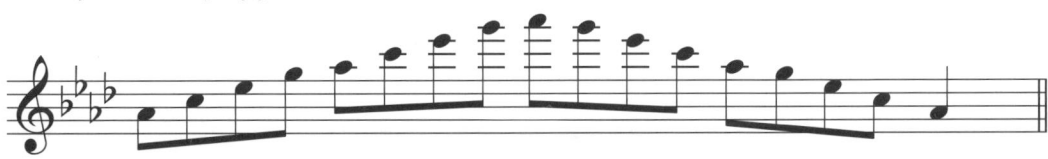

G# harmonic minor scale (two octaves)

G# melodic minor scale (two octaves)

G# minor arpeggio (two octaves)

A♭ pentatonic major scale (two octaves)*

55

Grade 8 continued

Dorian scale on A♭ (two octaves)*

G#/A♭ minor 7th arpeggio (two octaves)*

Mixolydian scale on A♭/G# (two octaves)*

A♭ major arpeggio with a lowered 7th (two octaves)

Diminished 7th arpeggio on A♭ (two octaves)‡